Written by Sally A Jones and Amanda C Jones
Illustrations and photographs by Sally A Jones

Published by GUINEA PIG EDUCATION

2 Cobs Way,
New Haw,
Addlestone,
Surrey,
KT15 3AF,
UK.
www.guineapigeducation.co.uk

ISBN: 978-0-9558315-0-8

Dear Kids,

If you want to aim for higher grades in your SATS or English exams read this book over and over again. Learn how to plan and order different kinds of stories, from adventure to ghost and mystery. Try using the ideas to write similar stories of your own. If you focus on all the points in this book you will soon be imagining splendid stories of your own. This book is a starting point to get you writing.

To Parents and Kids,

As a former class teacher working as a tutor for the 9-14 age range I am only too familiar with the problem children have expressing their ideas. They look at a title and their minds go blank. I have put together a collection of ideas for story writing to help these children. If, however, you have a child whose imagination runs wild, these stories will inspire him to start writing. Many of these stories have been put together by children studying English one to one. In our sessions we have explored characters, settings and different plots. We have discussed various endings to see which ones work for different stories. Children will identify with the ideas in this book.

Children must be encouraged to read but they don't always have the time. By saturating them with good ideas and vocabulary we can assist them in their writing and build on the work they do at school.

People have always made up stories. In early times before people could read, short stories were told and retold and passed down the generations as folk tales. Myths are also old stories about supernatural beings that were once believed. Legends, such as, George and the Dragon are stories which could have been true. Fables have a moral, which teach us a lesson. Do you remember how tortoise beat hare in the race? Can you think of more?

Everyone can remember some of the traditional stories they were told as small children, how about Red Riding Hood or the Three Billy Goats Gruff. These stories often use rhyme or repetition to help us remember them or join in. In the Three Little Pigs the big bad wolf <u>huffs</u> and he <u>puffs</u> and he blows the house down. The Billy Goats <u>trip</u> <u>trap</u>, <u>trip</u> <u>trap</u> over the iron bridge uses alliteration, (words beginning with the same sound) or onomatopoeia, (words that sound like the action), to create word pictures.

You may have seen a pantomime about a traditional story. Here is a modern shortened version of such a story based on a legend.

Once upon a time there was a boy named Dick Whittington. He decided to seek his fortune. As there was no public transport in those days, he left his hometown of Gloucester and set out for London Town on foot. Weary from his long walk, Dick sat down along the way and was befriended by a smart black cat. The two became such close friends that the cat decided to accompany Dick on his journey.

Dick found it difficult in the big city with no money, so he was forced to take a job at the king's palace. It was there that he fell absolutely head over heels in love with a beautiful girl. Her name was Alice but there was one difficulty, she was the king's daughter. Dick knew that he must win the king's favour to win the hand of this beautiful girl. However, there were those in the palace who did not like Dick. They saw his good intentions towards Alice. They were jealous. They thought what could we do? Eventually they came up with a plan to set up Dick. They hid one of Alice's precious necklaces in Jack's possessions so Dick was accused of being a thief. Then he was dismissed. In his grief he made the decision to return to Gloucester with his cat. As he reached the country he sat down to weep, but what was that? Dick heard the distant bells of London Town. They were saying clearly 'Go Back Dick Whittington, Go Back to London Town'

When he arrived back, he was reunited with Alice who told him she had found her necklace and had told the king of his innocence. The king gave Dick a job immediately on his ship. Of course, he took his cat. It was just as well because the ship had the most terrible problem with rats. They were everywhere, chewing all the ships provisions. What was worse, they had minds like humans and were plotting against the crew to take over the boat. They kidnapped poor Alice and locked her up. Then the ship hit a terrible storm and the whole crew were nearly ship wrecked. The cat was no fool because he set to work capturing every single rat and the king rat that was watching over Alice. In the end, Dick rescued Alice. On his return to London, the king was so grateful he gave his daughter's hand in marriage to Dick. He also bestowed upon him the title of Lord Mayor of London and the couple lived happily ever after

Now write your own traditional tale or fairy tale.

Story Planning

If you plan your story…

    You can organise it into paragraphs. When you start writing you will find it easier to put events in the right order. You will know what will happen. In your mind you will have a picture of the setting and the characters. You can start writing without worrying about what you are going to write and concentrate on spelling and punctuation.

    If you jot down notes for your plan under headings you can…

- get ideas down quickly before you forget
- refer to them quickly
- develop your ideas further as you write and as new ideas come to you.

Ask yourself…..

- What will happen in my story?
- When will it happen?
- How will it happen?
- What is the weather like?

- Who is there?
- When do they meet?
- How do they react to each other?
- How do they feel, behave, and think about events?
- What decisions do they make?
- What is the result of these decisions on others?

- How will the events unfold in my story?
- What will these events lead to?
- Is there suspense making the reader want to read on?
- Does it lead to an exciting climax?
- Is there a satisfactory conclusion?

When you make a plan don't write your whole story on the sheet but focus on the main, key points.

- Writing a plan helps you decide on the order of the story.

When you start to write, the plan will help you remember…

* How the story begins
* What happens?
* How the story will end
* About characters
* Settings

Plan a Story

Decide…

* if the story will be written in the first or third person,
* if you are the hero or heroine,
* or if it is told by a narrator.

Who the main
characters are…

* Consider their names
* What they look like
* What their personality is like
* How they behave – fearful, tired, hopeless, courageous, strong etc.
* How they get on with other characters

The story is set in…

* details of the place

The story begins by…

* The first line sets the scene and tells you what the story will be about.
* Introduce characters, settings, and plot

This happens first…

and after that…

* develop ideas in plot
* develop characters

and then…

* Introduce dialogue, but take care with punctuation.

The most exciting
happening or climax is…

The story ends – make
sure your ending is not
too far fetched!

* The reader will not believe in too fantastic an ending and be disappointed.

> **<u>When you are planning a story make notes on setting, character and plot.</u>**
>
> **Write just enough detail to help you – but not too much. You can develop ideas as you write STORY PLANS.**

You may be familiar with the story of Joseph in The Bible.

Stories can have more than one setting	* A field in the land of Canaan where Joseph is a shepherd * A wealthy merchant's house in Egypt where Joseph is a slave * The dark, dingy prison where Joseph is a prisoner in chains * Pharaoh's palace in Egypt
Some details about characters	* Joseph – the second youngest of Jacob's twelve sons * Benjamin the youngest son of Jacob * Ten brothers of Joseph – very jealous * Jacob – Joseph's father * Potiphar and his wife – a rich merchant who buys Joseph as a slave * A butler and a baker – fellow prisoners with Joseph whose dreams he interprets * Pharaoh – the ruler of Egypt, who has disturbing dreams

Plot
The order of events in the story

Introduction (the story begins)

- Jacob gives his favourite son Joseph a coat of many colours.
- His jealous brothers attack him, strip him of his coat, nearly throw him in a pit, sell him to some passing traders as a slave, tell their father of Joseph's death
- Joseph is sold to a rich merchant Potiphar.

Middle Paragraph

- He throws Joseph into prison
- Joseph explains the meanings of other prisoners' dreams.
- Pharaoh is disturbed by dreadful dreams – he hears that there is a man in prison who explains dreams. He sends for Joseph. Joseph tells Pharaoh what the dreams mean. In return he is given a good position at the palace – becomes rich.

How the story ends

- Joseph's family leave Canaan because there is a famine – to seek food in Egypt.
- The brothers meet Joseph but they don't recognise him. He gives them corn – plants a gold cup in Benjamin's bag.
- Brothers take the blame for the theft when Benjamin is accused. "Not Him" they say.
- Joseph sees his brothers have changed and forgives them.
- He reveals who he is.
- Happy ending

Use good adjectives and adverbs to write interesting sentences.

- A fox crept softly into the garden.

- A fox crept cunningly into the garden in the depths of night.

- At dawn, a fox prowled cunningly in the garden

- At dawn, a fox prowled cunningly through the hole in the garden fence and made his way to the chicken run.

Don't use sentences, which are too long or have too many good words.
GET THE BALANCE RIGHT.

<u>Now finish the sentences to write an animal story</u>

At dawn a fox crept cunningly through the hole in the garden fence and made his way to the chicken run. There was a terrible………………………………
and the fox………………………..………………………
When Tom woke up Aunt Jo was …………………….…
…………………………………………………………..
Uncle Bert muttered,
"……………………………………………………………"

After breakfast Tom decided to go to the woods to ………………………………………………………
He spotted the fox and……………………………………
………………………………………………………………
For a moment they both….………………………………
Then…………………………………………………………

Suddenly in the distance Tom saw another sight that made his heart beat faster. It was his…………..
………………………………………………………………..
Uncle Bert had not seen Tom but he had seen the fox.
He picked up his gun………………………………………
Tom…………………………………………………………
………………………………………………………………
In surprise Uncle Bert……………………………………
The fox…………………………………………….........
………………………………………………………………

The White Fox

At dawn a fox prowled cunningly through the hole in the garden fence and made his way to the chicken run. There was a terrible squawking as the chickens saw the predator before them. Then, with one swift movement the fox pounced and his jaws closed round the neck of a bird. Swiftly, he lifted the chicken and carried it back to his den. When Tom woke up Aunt Jo was in a panic. She had collected the eggs to find her prize hen had gone.

After breakfast Tom decided to go to the woods to search for the fox. Over the meal Tom had listened to his Uncle Bert describe a huge white fox he had seen in the area the week before. Uncle Bert had sworn that he was going to get that beast at any cost. "He won't have any more of our hens," he uttered between clenched teeth. As Tom crept through the twisty woodland path, overgrown by shrubs, he peered into every hole but he couldn't find any signs of the fox. He searched the forest floor but there were no tracks. A little disheartened, he decided to give up and go home. Then as he turned around, his heart missed a beat. There, in front of him was a handsome white fox. For a moment they both froze and stared at each other. Then it made a bolt in the other direction. Tom ran in an attempt to follow it but it was outrunning him.

Tom continued to track the fox for what seemed like an hour, though it was probably only a few minutes. He wasn't going to let the creature get away without a good look. Suddenly in the distance Tom saw another sight that made his heart pound. It was his Uncle Bert crouching in the hedgerow with his gun. It was pointed at something. As Tom looked closer (peered into the distance) he could see the white fox feeding on some chicken bones with her three cubs. Tom's mind raced. He didn't have time to think. He just sprinted forward screaming.
"Hello, Uncle Bert, What are you doing?" In surprise the man lost his grip of the gun and it lurched upwards firing a shot into the air. The fox and her babies disappeared into the depths of the forest and were never seen again.

LETS LOOK AT A GHOST STORY

Setting	old house, derelict, empty, overgrown, crumbling
Characters	I, cat, feeling of ghosts
Order of events (Introduction)	* the character walks in the country * comes across a derelict, empty house * tempted to explore
How the plot continues	* door slams shut * alone in the dusty, dirty, broken down house, full of cobwebs and spiders * hears footsteps upstairs * panics, tries to escape * wakes up outside, looks back but sees only a cat
How the story ends on a Cliff hanger	* hammers on door * won't open * hand on shoulder * everything goes blank…

A Creepy Tale

Is anyone there?
Use words to create atmosphere.

It was a moonlit evening so I decided to go for a walk by the river. As I strolled along whistling to myself, I stopped to look at the creepy old lodge house, which had stood empty for many years. People told of strange goings on in the house. It had fallen into a derelict state with crumbling walls and peeling paintwork. There was a gaping hole in the roof where tiles had blown off in the winter gales. The garden was a tangle of overgrown shrubs and trees where roots had broken up the path.

As I am curious by nature I ambled up the path, picking my way through the piles of rotting wood and leaves and pushed on the old oak door. It creaked as it opened. The lock had been forced. I stuck my head round crying,
"Is anyone there?" There was only an eerie silence so I stepped into the hall. The pungent odour of damp made me sneeze. The cobwebs hung like lanterns in

the hall, glistening in the shafts of moonlight from the door. A sudden bang made me jump. It was the door closing. Determined to be brave I peered cautiously into every room. Then I heard another thump on the landing above me, which sent shivers down my spine.
It sounded again and again, like footsteps coming slowly down the steep flight of stairs. Panic seized my body. My only wish was to leave that place as quickly as possible but I was frozen to the spot by fear. Who was up there? I asked myself. How could I escape? My heart beat faster. I thought I would faint. Gaining my strength I made a dash for the old door, but as I grappled with the lock it stuck fast. I pulled and pushed at it but it would not budge. (The writer builds up suspense. He's trapped!). Then I felt a cold touch on me. I screamed for help.

I didn't know how long I had sat dozing under the apple tree by the gate. When my eyes flickered open I saw the old house frowning down at me. I remembered the dream of how I had been trying to escape through a door that was locked but someone opened it for me. I had run so fast that I tripped over the twisty roots that had overgrown the path. Everything had gone black for a second but someone had helped me up and spoken kindly to me. I wanted to thank them but as I looked back all I saw was a black cat staring at me with green eyes from the step.

The Rescue

After school, Tom tiptoed cautiously up the overgrown path and rattled the heavy doorknocker but there was no reply. Nervously, he pushed the crumpled envelope through the rusty letterbox and ran back to the iron gate. Jumping on his bike, he sped off down the road not daring to look back. Old Mr Evans stooped down to pick up the letter and tore it open with his wrinkled hands. His face frowned as he read the scribbled note. Please Sir can I have my cat back?

Later that evening as Tom watched TV, Tom's mum handed him the old man's reply. He read it aloud, "Certainly not! Your cat has done damage to my flowerbeds. He is safe in my house locked in a cage where he can't do any further damage. You must pay £100 damages to get him back."
Tom's Mum watched her son's pale face flare up with anger as he rose up hurriedly, grabbed his anorak and headed for the door.
"Where are you going Tom?" she asked anxiously but did not receive a reply. Down the road he ran not stopping until he reached the forbidding looking grey stone house. Outside, he paused and looked. He observed the side window was open. As darkness fell Tom crept silently like a mouse down the overgrown passage. He climbed the drainpipe and slipped through the window. Now he was standing in the hallway. He heard a feeble meow coming
from the next room, as if the animal sensed that help was near. Tom moved on cautiously trying to avoid the tiniest sound. Then he stepped on a creaky floorboard. He froze! He heard the sound of footsteps. The old man sensed an intruder and was coming down the stairs. Tom ducked into a cupboard and froze.

As old Mr Evans stumbled into the kitchen Tom's heart beat so loudly, he thought it would give him away. Mr Evans was quite deaf and after a quick search round he satisfied himself that all was secure. After uttering "Shut up you horrid creature," to the cat he returned to his drawing room to doze in the chair. Seizing his chance, Tom stole quietly into the kitchen. Seeing his precious pet, his nimble hands flicked open the lock and grabbed his cat. Grabbing a towel, he wrapped the cat up and raced towards the door. He flung it open and headed down the path. Confused by the noise the old man shuffled back into the kitchen. Tom heard his angry cry but the words were lost in the wind.

The opening sentence grabs attention and creates suspense. Key information is held back that was mentioned in the 1st sentence.

Thrillers use the technique of telling us something and making us wait.

The writer introduces two different characters from different backgrounds that feel real. We wonder how they will be brought together and connected.

Planning a rescue story

Trapped

Settings…

Characters…

1) * Peter on holiday with friends – age 15
    * In his spare time goes for a walk taking sandwiches
    * Explores the long sandy beaches
    * Walks for hours amongst the rock pools looking for shells
    * Swims, eats lunch, reads book

2) * Settles himself down in a little cove
    * Starts to doze
    * Doesn't see tide coming in
    * Turns to go back – cut off – tide in
    * No path along beach – panic no way up cliffs
    * Only steep cliff – sits on rock – panic, fear as sea comes in around him

3) * Friends alert police
    * Boy missing
    * Rescue party set out
    * Launch lifeboat or helicopter rescue
    * Meanwhile Peter clings to rock in hopeless despair

* Helicopter spots Peter – a small figure of boy on rock below
* Radios mainland
* Launch rescue attempt
* Hauled up by ropes
* Glad to be safe with friends, will not go out alone again

The following rescue story teaches you to make your writing more interesting.

* The **characters** are Jasmit, his Dad and the Major

* The **setting** is a seaside town at half term

A brief outline of the plot would include:

1) * Jasmit decides to go rock pooling at half term. He meets the Major at the harbour who asks him to help on his boat but he declines.
   * Tells Jasmit to take care

2) * Jasmit gets carried away and walks too far around the point.
   * Gets cut off by the tide
   * Filled with horror
   * Darkness falls
   * Screams for help

3) * After some time Dad and Major rescues him in a rowing boat.
   * Tells him to take their advice next time   he goes out walking alone on the beach.

Trapped

Jasmit was on half term holiday. As his parents had gone shopping, he decided to take a stroll by the sea. He packed his stereo, a lunch consisting of crisps, pasta salad, a banana and a bottle of water and put them in his rucksack. He set off along the sea wall. Passing 'Sea Mist' moored in the harbour. He cried out,

"Hello Major."

"Hello, young man. You've got some spare time have you? Come and help me paint my boat." Jasmit pulled a funny face.

" Sorry I've no time. I'm walking round the point to look for crabs and things."

"You take care," replied the old man.

"Remember the tides come in quickly in these parts." He watched Jasmit's solitary figure disappear into the distance as he walked along the sandy beach to the point.

Jasmit had spent two enjoyable hours poking about in the rock pools. He had found lots of little hermit crabs and raced them against each other, watching them come in and out of their shells. He was into biology. When he grew up he planned to become a marine biologist. It was hot work. He sat

down in the warm sun to rest. Two hours later he woke up with a start. He could hear the sound of

waves lapping very close to him. He looked around in horror. There was sea surrounding him on every

side and it dawned on him that the tide had come in. Jasmit stood up on the rocks and looked for an escape route. He was cut off. He could not climb the cliffs because they were too steep. A feeling of panic filled him. Now he would be stuck here all night, which was a terrifying thought and made him tremble all over. Jasmit screamed out,
"HELP! HELP!" over and over again but only the squawking sea gulls seemed to hear his cry. He waved his anorak in the air to distant ships but he remained unnoticed.

Alone, marooned on his little rock, Jasmit felt frightened and alone. As darkness gathered everything took on an eerie tone. He started to imagine tomorrow's headlines and it made him feel dizzy. He felt himself faint to the ground. Suddenly, in a state of half consciousness a new sound caught his ear. It was the familiar sound of an engine chugging and there was the smell of new paint that made him feel safe again. At that moment a pair of familiar hands closed around him and pulled him into the boat. He heard Dad's kind voice say, "Jasmit, we've been so worried!" Then he heard the voice of the Major,
"You didn't listen to my advice did you? Next time you have spare time stay and help me on my boat."
Knowing he was safe Jasmit slept all the way back to the harbour.

Better Sentences

Simple Sentences

A boy was on holiday.

He decided to take a stroll by the sea.

Jasmit searched the rock pools for crabs.

Compound Sentences

The Major stood there with his binoculars **but** he could not spot Jasmit.

They jumped in the boat **and** sailed out to sea.

Jasmit cried for help **until** his voice became hoarse.

Complex Sentence

Knowing he was safe, he slept in the boat all the way back to the harbour.

Far out to sea, there was a boat with people but Jasmit was not on it.

Jasmit, who was a brave boy, felt afraid when he found he was cut off by the tides

Complex Sentence with Speech

"Where do you think he could be?" asked Dad nervously.

"I think we should search for him," suggested the Major, "it's not like him to stay out in the sun all afternoon."

Sailing near the rocks Dad cried,
"Look! There's Jasmit's jumper!"

Always remember to punctuate your work!

Correct the following paragraph using the appropriate punctuation. Then turn to the following page to see if you are right!

jasmit was on half term holiday as his parents had gone shopping he thought he would take a walk by the sea he put his stereo and a packed lunch of crisps a pasta salad a banana and a bottle of water in his rucksack and set off on his way as jasmit passed sea mist moored by the harbour wall he said a cheery hello to mr smith who was painting his boat ready for summer hi young man are you off for a walk yes I thought id walk round the point theres some big crabs and things you watch out remember the tides can catch you out.

Punctuation - . , ? "....." A

.   **Full stops** always end a sentence.

,   **Commas** separate words in a list, clauses or parts of a sentence. (There is never a comma before and)

"   **Speech marks** begin and end speech.

    A new sentence, names and places always start with a **capital letter**.

Jasmit was on half term holiday. As his parents had gone shopping, he though he would take a walk by the sea. He put his stereo and a packed lunch of crisps, a pasta salad, a banana and a bottle of water in his rucksack and set off on his way. As Jasmit passed 'Sea Mist' moored by the harbour wall, he said a cheery hello to Mr Smith, who was painting his boat ready for summer.

"Hi young man. Are you off for a walk?"

"Yes, I thought I'd walk round the point. There are some big crabs and things."

"You watch out! Remember the tides can catch you out."

Choose a narrator

Shall I choose?

First person - I
As I left the harbour I heard a shout from the white boat.

3rd Person - He/She, Jasmit
As Jasmit passed the harbour, he heard a shout from the white boat.

Remember, always keep the same narrator don't swap!

When the main character tells the story he can use his own dialogue to tell what kind of person he is.

"Jasmit, Where are you off to?"
I heard a voice call my name. I glanced in the direction of the boat. I'm the sort of boy who likes his own company so when I have time to myself I normally pretend to be in a hurry.
"Are you off school today with time on your hands? Have you got a spare hour to help me paint my boat? I could do with some help lad."
I want to know why adults always think you should be doing something. They don't realise that kids sometimes need a bit of space. Avoiding the old man's look I mumbled a reply,
"I'm sorry Major I'm off to look for crabs and things for my school project."

Speakers move the story along.

"I think he's cut off," said the Major. Jasmit had walked along the beach to the point over six hours ago. The tide had turned and the waves were now lapping over the shingle beach. "Let's wait for another five minutes," suggested Dad. He may have gone into the village. The kind Major was a retired man with a snowy white tuft of hair who was a skilled sailor and took on the role of lifeguard to the local children.
"I think we should take Sea Mist out to look for him. I've been painting the boat all afternoon I'm sure I wouldn't have missed him go by." Dad and the Major jumped aboard Sea Mist and started the engine swiftly. The old man steered the boat out to sea and headed in the direction of the point. As they turned the corner Dad cried,
"Listen! I thought I heard Jasmit shouting." They listened but the voice was lost in the squawking of the seagulls. They chugged on through the rolling waves but there was no sign of Jasmit. As they turned there was the steep familiar row of black rocks of the point. At that moment they spotted a small solitary figure waving….

Look the plot unfolds using - description of characters and setting, dialogue and narrative all in one piece of writing.

Building up settings and characters.

Begin with describing the setting.

Jasmit's home was in a small seaside town in Sussex. There was a little harbour with brightly coloured boats that bobbed up and down on the tide. Jasmit knew the owners, like Major Smith. Sometimes during the holidays Jasmit would go down to the harbour and chat to the old man as he pottered about. Then, at low tide he would wander aimlessly along the beach with his net, breathing in the salty air of seaweed. He would spend a few hours at the rock point searching the soft sand for crabs and other creatures. One day he hoped to be a marine biologist.

Characters

Give 2 or 3 details about the way the character looks.

Jasmit was a serious boy with a mop of untidy black hair. In his spare time he liked to explore the beach. He would search the sand for crabs and other sea creatures. In his room he had a vast collection of books about marine life. He said he wanted to be a marine biologist when he grew up.

More Sentences
Remember vary the lengths of your sentences.
Use some simple, some compound and some complex.

Lots of short sentences are dull. Always make use of 3 types of sentence, strong verbs, adjectives and adverbs.

Simple Sentence

Jasmit was a boy.
Jasmit was an intelligent, serious boy.

Compound Sentence (add a connective or conjunction)

Jasmit lived in a small seaside town and there was a little harbour with brightly coloured boats.
He strolled briskly down to the beach because he wanted to search for fat crabs at low tide.

Complex Sentences

Jasmit searched the rocks, which were covered in seaweed.
Jasmit, who wanted to be a marine biologist, searched the rocks for creatures.
As Jasmit turned round, he saw that he was completely cut off by the tide.
Despite screaming for help, the tide came in and he was trapped on the rocks.

Some children were asked to write a paragraph remembering the time when they wanted a special pet. A family member brought home the pet as a surprise in a box.

Persuading people to read on

It had been my dream to have a dog. I asked my mum for one. One day she came home from work with a box. Inside it there was a puppy. I was so happy. **(James)**
(not so interesting!)

It had been my dream to have an amazingly cute puppy. I had been nagging my mum for weeks to get one. Then one day my mum came home from work. I was upstairs. All I heard was a bark. I couldn't believe it. Is this really why she was late home? I rushed downstairs at top speed nearly falling and breaking my neck but luckily I just skidded along the floor. I came face to face with my dream. Was it true? Was it a pretend joke or was I daydreaming? No it was definitely here along with the lead, cage and bowls and everything. I was so pleased I ran around screaming the good news. **(Sophie)**
(more interesting)

For months it had been my dream to have a little puppy. I kept pointing out to Dad all the different sorts of dogs. When we went for a drive, I'd plead,
"Dad, can I have a cute little dog like that one?" I don't know what made dad finally listen but I remember clearly that September evening. The car pulled into the drive. Dad

was very late. He opened the passenger door and took a large cardboard box. He carefully carried it up the path. I raced down stairs to open the door. I asked in a curious tone,

"What's in that box?" expecting it to be filled with old files from work. I could see from dad's face that something had happened. He looked at me with a strange sort of smile on his face. I peered into the box. I gasped in amazement. Was this why dad was late? Had my dream come true or was I daydreaming. In the box was my puppy. **(Lucy)**

(keeps the readers interest so he wants to find out more)

The last three paragraphs help you develop your writing and attain higher grades. Paragraph 3 shows how you can organise your work to make it interesting and convincing so the reader wants to read on. It shows how you can hold back the information until the end of the paragraph to build up suspense. Words like 'plead' or 'beg' are the right words here. They are more interesting than 'say'. **Use the right words and avoid cluttering up your work with too many words that don't fit in**. Put in little details about people and the way they feel and look, like "mum's strange sort of smile" or the description of the driveway. These help the reader to get involved so they want to find out more. Don't forget you can always use humour or dialogue. Remember people have different ways of talking.

Revision

You know that a story needs…
* A plot
* A sequence of events that unfolds through the story
* To be organised into a beginning a middle and an end.

To make a good story you also need…
* Narrative (a narrator telling a story)
* Description
* Speech

Writers have to…
*Think about their audience, the age and background of their readers
*Gain the reader's interest and draw them into the story
*Create a sense of tension or suspense
*Make us feel involved so we want to read on
*Help us know the characters so we raise questions in our minds about them and where they fit into the story.

The Barbecue

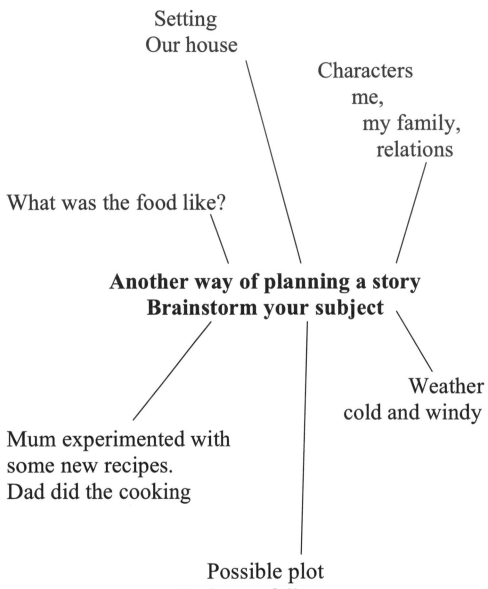

Setting
Our house

Characters
me,
   my family,
     relations

What was the food like?

Another way of planning a story
Brainstorm your subject

Weather
cold and windy

Mum experimented with
some new recipes.
Dad did the cooking

Possible plot
Barbecue falls over
Food burnt, Fire
or
Cat jumps on barbecue to get a sausage, knocks it over,
causes fire, gets burnt and taken to vet.

The Barbecue

I felt uneasy as the clock chimed six and the guests started to arrive. My parents had been planning the barbecue for months and now it was blazing. The aroma of frying burgers drifted across the garden. The cling foil covers of the salads were blowing in the breeze. Dad was positioned as chef with the tongs and Mum appeared with the steaming pots of ready cooked chicken to brown on the barbecue. There was a knock on the door.

For some time I had felt a bit reluctant about this occasion because Mum had invited relations we hadn't seen for months.

Can you finish the story?

Believable characters

Who came to the barbecue?

For some time I had felt a bit reluctant about this occasion because Mum had invited relations we hadn't seen for months. As I strolled towards the front door I felt awkward and wondered what I would say to Great Aunt Margaret and Uncle Bill. I shouldn't have worried because there wasn't an opportunity to say more than a quick, "Hello." The enormous figure of my aunt threw her arms around me and hugged me so tight I felt short of breath. Then my uncle shook my hand so hard I felt it would drop off and without further invitation they strolled straight through into the garden. I heard my aunts booming voice say,
"How lovely to see you my dear after all this time"
I was about to shut the door when I observed my mother's cousin screech to a halt outside. She raced in and smothered me with kisses on each cheek. She threw a huge bar of chocolate into my hand and went on through to the garden. She was followed by her silent husband and her three sullen children, in their best outfits. Everybody had arrived so I closed the door.

When characters in a story speak to each other, the writer can show what they are thinking and feeling and how they react to each other. As the characters discuss things, they help the reader make discoveries about what is going to happen in the plot. Every line of dialogue can move the story on.

Planning a Story
The Bullies

Settings…
Characters…

1)
* The scream echoed through the alleyway
* Stacey pulled Rashpal's hair
* Grabbed her diary
* Janet took it and started to read it
* Her face turned into a sneer as she threw it into the mud
* She says, "Oh so you hate Stacey and I do you?"
* She comes nearer to Rashpal and her hand comes out in a menacing way

2)
* Rashpal pushes Janet/Stacey - she starts to run very fast
* Stacey says, "Janet lets get that girl and teach her a lesson."
* They start to chase her
* Rashpal is terrified
* She dashes across the road not seeing a bike approaching
* It hits the girl knocking her down
* She lies on the road
* Stacey and Janet are frightened that she is badly injured – they disappear quickly

3)
* An ambulance is called
* The girl is taken to hospital
* Her mum arrives with a police lady
* They ask Rashpal why she ran across the road without looking
* She told them what had happened
* The next day the police lady visits the school to talk to the children about bullying
* They have a description of the two girls
* They take them out of the class to talk to them about the trouble they've caused
* What will happen if they bully another person again?
* The girls are ashamed of their ways and promise not to behave like this again

The Chase

At home time the children of Row Town High poured out wildly onto the pavement shouting at each other and waving their bags in the air.

"Hi Jo, Have you heard about the fight?"

"No, what's happening."

"It's that spiteful girl Stacey. She's threatening to beat up Rashpal!"

"Why what's she supposed to have done?" uttered Lois in surprise.

"Apparently Rashpal has written I hate Stacey in her diary. We'd better get over there and help her immediately." The girls broke into a run and hurried down the road to the alley that cut through the estate.

Stacey had Rashpal pinned against the wall.

"So you hate me do you?" screamed the school bully.

"Leave me alone and get your hands off me."

"Hand over your diary. Let's see what you've written down about me."

"Keep your hands off. It's private." Stacey approached Rashpal in a menacing way with her hand grasping the diary. In return, Rashpal struggled to get away and started to run. Then Stacey and her gang started to pursue her. Faster and faster they all ran calling out names and threats. Rashpal panicked. She darted across the road. There was a terrifying screech of brakes, which was followed by an awful moment of silence and the girl lay on the road, her face as white as chalk.

After that everything stopped. The car drivers and pedestrians all stared in horror. A huge crowd gathered around the injured girl. A kindly bystander covered her in a blanket until the ambulance arrived to take her to hospital. Soon the familiar sound of a police car could be heard. The police arrived on the scene but the bullies had disappeared. They started to chat to witnesses.

"We can help," said Jo bravely.

"We know this girl called Stacey and her gang. She's made Rashpal's life really difficult. She was running away from them when this awful thing happened".

The policewoman wrote everything down. The next morning the head teacher of Row Town High looked very solemn. She said it was a very sad day for the school because a group of girls had been suspended. She hoped it would never happen again.

Stories can start in different ways

The Rescue story starts with a description, which sets the scene, whereas the bully story goes straight into the action. We don't find out at first why there is a fight or what the relationship is between the girls. The plot evolves during the story.

Setting

Look at the picture.   **Write the first paragraph of a story using the picture to set the scene.**

Think of a title for this story…

Did anyone see anything?

What happened when they all went home?

As the sun set over the mountains, the sky had a golden glow. The lake was calm. Shiny black rocks glistened in the water. A thin mist shrouded the mountaintops. I was enjoying my evening walk by the lake.

Suddenly my attention was caught by a dark shape looming up in the distance. It looked like…..

Read through the following questions and answers and then write a middle paragraph and an ending.

Dilemma

What did it look like?

It was the size of a dinosaur with huge limbs and a massive tail that was as long as the rest of its body. It looked like something out of a museum.

What did it do?

It swam towards me for a while getting bigger but then it disappeared and I lost sight of it. Its huge form made ripples across the water like a paddle steamer.

Did it make any noise?

No! It came silently and slowly; only the splashing sound of the waves against the rocks reached my ears.

How did it move?

It swam slowly moving its powerful body through the water.

What did you feel when you saw this creature?

I was staggered because I have lived here all my life and I've never seen anything like it before. I was a bit frightened, amazed and terrified when it kept coming towards me. My hands were shaking.

Climax

What did you do next?

I grabbed my camera and took a shot. When I lost sight of it I raced home and phoned the editor of our local paper. A team of reporters came straight away. Then a T.V crew came up to the loch.

What was the scene like then?

Thousands of people came with their cameras hoping to see something.

A first draft from a child's work:

<u>The Monster</u>

As the sun set over the mountains, the sky had a golden glow. The lake was calm. The rocks glistened in the water. A thin mist shrouded the mountaintops. I was enjoying my evening walk by the lake.

As my eyes looked across the water a dark shape loomed in the distance. It caught my attention. I stood on a shiny, black rock to get a closer view. I could now see the enormous monster had dark brown skin with vivid orange stripes. A long thin tail swayed above the monster's head, spraying tiny water droplets in all directions. It was amazing. The monster started moving across the lake with its powerful body gliding through the freezing water. Suddenly, it dived down deep and I lost sight of it. Then, leaping up it jumped right out of the water and shone in the evening sun.

My camera clicked and took a first class picture. I raced home as fast as I could and rang the newspaper. My picture appeared on the front page. Thousands of people went down to the loch. They were holding up their digital cameras hoping to get a glimpse of the Loch ness monster. Did they get the pictures they so longed for, evidence to show the creature did exist? Not surprisingly, he had completely disappeared. Everyone started to speculate. Had he returned to his home deep under the water? Was the monster only to be seen every hundred years or had I dreamed the whole thing?

* Don't overuse adjectives, use the right ones

* Don't repeat words

* Proof read your work, always read your work through.

* Write out a second draft published copy.

The Unexpected Visitor

"Help me Mum," I screamed.
"There's a spider. Come and catch it!"
I don't know why but I've never liked creepy crawlies.
They always send me running. If I see a spider suddenly
jump out at me I yell so loudly.
"What do you want now, Susie? I've got to go to work.
You're not a baby anymore so you shouldn't be making
all that fuss over a tiny little insect."
As far as I was concerned these horrible creatures made
a point of searching me out. They were always in my
room and not my brother's. Mum, said it was because
my room was a tip but I think they're attracted to me
because they know I'm terrified.

This was the largest spider I'd ever seen, crouching
in front of my wardrobe. It was staring at me. It was
thinking what fun for a little spider to have such power
over this huge human child. What a good opportunity I
have chosen to come out when this girl is tidying her
wardrobe and there is all this clutter around. In return I
fixed my eyes on him so he did not try to hide in some
secret place where I would not find him. Then, I'd be
lying there at night wondering where he was lurking or
when he might show up. I'd have to do it I thought.
Trembling with fear I grabbed a container from the
dressing table and at last I summoned all

my courage to move in on him. Creeping forward, my hand came down slowly with the container to trap him so he could not escape. Sensing danger, the spider made a dash. He scuttled forwards towards me, jumping on the bed I screamed and he disappeared.

At that moment my big brothers angry, red face appeared round the door.
"What's going on this time?" he roared.
"There's a spider in there I yelled," pointing at the boxes.
"Oh, some little speck I expect," he sneered,
"Why don't you grow up?" He went down on his hands and knees and started to overturn everything frantically in his search to find it.
"Found it," he gasped in surprise and stepping back,
"It's a big one, better get a tissue." He ran off only to appear a second later. Making a grab he ran down the stairs two at a time and ran through the door. A few minutes later he returned,
"Couldn't kill it," he said, "I've taken it down the road."
"I thought you didn't like picking them up," I said.
"You've got to overcome all these silly fears," he replied. For the first time I wanted to hug my brother but I just mumbled thanks. It was the bravest thing he'd ever done for me.

A Fright!

    As I observed the shopping list before me I saw that we required some bananas from the green grocers. A few minutes later I propped my bike up against the shop window and went inside with my list. It was warmer inside the shop so I took off my gloves and started to search through the bananas. My Mum preferred bananas to be a certain size and not too ripe. At the back there was just the right bunch. I picked it up and put it in the basket.

    Suddenly, I went stiff with fright and my heart almost missed a beat. Only a few inches from my hand, perched on the banana was an enormous yellow spider. The most terrifying looking creature I had ever seen. It was not the usual sort of spider you find in the garden shed at home. This was a most unusual specimen of the sort you might find in a tropical country. Could this spider have come from the banana plantations of Jamaica? I shuddered as I stared down at it and my hand trembled. Tropical spiders can be lethal I thought. They have a poisonous sting………

Finish the story

Possible endings
* The girl is bitten by the spider and becomes very sick.
* The girl seeks the store manager and an expert in tropical insects is called in to take the spider to the local zoo.
* The girl panics and runs from the shop. She later reads that someone was bitten and she feels awful that she did not report the incident.

The Flood

I switched off the light and lay in the dark listening to the rain lashing on my bedroom window. The wind howled like an angry monster, whipping up the sea, so that the waves crashed furiously onto the shore. I attempted to sleep trying to ignore the noise of wind and rain. I had lived by the sea for as long as I could remember so I was used to the gales that blew up and down the coast all winter long.

Then there came the wildest wind and heaviest rain at the height of the storm. There was a blinding flash of lightning a loud clap of thunder. At that same moment I heard a human cry that filled me with terror,
"Oh no," came the voice from a downstairs room.
"The water is coming through the door," continued the voice in some distress.
"The tide is still rising. It won't be high tide until eleven o'clock."……

Continue the middle paragraph and write the ending.

The Storm

I switched off the light and lay in the dark, listening to the heavy rain lashing against my bedroom window. The wind howled like an angry monster tearing at the branches of the tree in my garden and knocking over everything in its path. I snuggled down under the duvet, burying my face into the pillow but there was to be no escape from the noise of wind and rain. It seemed ages before I dozed off, only to be awakened again a few minutes later, by the clatter of a dustbin lid blowing down the street, the banging of an unlatched gate and the crashing over of empty milk bottles on the step.

As I lay staring into the darkness, there came the wildest winds and the remaining leaves on the tree were ferociously tossed and torn by the wind. The twigs on the trees snapped off and hurtled towards my window. Suddenly I sat upright in my bed. There was a terrifying cracking sound and then an awful crash. It was followed by an eerie silence. The old tree had come down and was sprawled on the grass.

Next morning when I awoke the wind had calmed down and light streamed into my window. Sadly, I remembered the events of the night. I was filled with remorse. I remembered the hot summer days when I had scaled the old trunk and sat in its leafy branches and played hide and seek with my brothers and sisters. For hours I had hidden there making plans and secret codes. Then I heard Dad's voice,
"Come and give me a hand children. The garden needs tidying up after the storm." I hurried down to help Dad collect up wood. It didn't go to waste. We used it to make an enormous bonfire with a guy on firework night. I also planted an apple pip, which grew into an even finer tree.

A family are halfway up a mountain when the car breaks down. They have no mobile phone. It's getting dark.

They spend an uncomfortable night on the mountain. They didn't tell anyone they were taking this route.

Which Ending?

* A happy ending where everything works out…

They walk to a service station to get help and supplies. A rescue vehicle comes.

* A cliff-hanger ending…

Two of the party go for help leaving the others wondering if they'll get back…

* An ending with some moral or lesson to be learnt, i.e. take the right equipment and always tell people where you're going.

Someone gets ill. They're left for days before help comes.

Sir Edmund Hilary and his guide Tenzing Norgay of Nepal were the first men to climb to the summit of Mount Everest, the world's highest mountain peak. Mount Everest is found in Central Asia on the borders of Nepal and China in the Himalayan mountain range. The peak is estimated to be 8848 metres above sea level! Sir Edmund reached the summit on May 29th 1953 he was knighted by the Queen for his achievement later that year.

Numerous explorers had made previous attempts to reach the summit of Mount Everest but all had failed. In fact, in 1922, an avalanche killed seven climbers. Moreover, in 1924 another group was believed to have reached the summit but were never seen again after a mist surrounded the mountain.

Such stories highlight just how dangerous such a climb is. Mountains are extremely hostile environments. High on the mountaintop it is so cold that plants cannot grow. There is only snow and bare rock. Sir Edmund and his companion would have had to survive freezing temperatures and weeks of suffering during their mission.

Finish writing the story called,

The Day I reached The Top Of The World

Firstly, read through the article about Sir Edmund Hilary, the first man to reach the summit of Mount Everest. Put yourself in his shoes. Use your imagination!

Paragraph One

Set the scene, describing the terrible conditions on the mountain.

Paragraph Two

Continue the account of your dangerous climb, for example, the problems you may have encountered with your guide Tenzing Norgay.

Paragraph Three

You reach the top.

Describe the excitement and joy you feel in having conquered this mountain. Finish by describing how you were knighted by the Queen for your achievement.

Remember; write three paragraphs each about the same length.

The First Time

The huge shape of the wheel came into view and I froze in my seat as a sensation of fear filled me. I was overwhelmed with terror as I saw it there, overshadowing the sparkling river in the August sunshine. I knew I had to go through with it or the family would call me a coward. As we drove close my heart started to beat faster, I felt a sickly feeling of butterflies in my stomach but Mum and Dad were too preoccupied with finding a parking space to notice my pale face.

"What do you think", said my Mum to my Dad. "Shall we wait in this queue?" I felt a moment of relief. Dad's reply sent prickly shivers down my spine.
"This is something we've wanted to do since it opened. Let's go for it! Anyway, the queue's moving quite fast."
Then he added,
"Are you excited, Kids?" My brother and sisters were so high, talking so loudly that my parents didn't notice the little shake of my head I gave in return. To my horror the queue moved swiftly on. Soon I found myself on the platform, with one-foot forward ready to hop on to the moving carriage. Now I was on
board the wheel, slowly moving up and up, leaving the ground behind. As the buildings and people below became small like a swarm of ants I clung to my seat in the middle of the carriage, not daring to move, unable to

cope with looking down. How can they stand on the edge taking photos like that, I thought? I hate heights.

Slowly the wheel turned, revolving ever so gently round and round. Higher soared my carriage to the top, as it looked down over the city – to the north the airport, the south the downs. Then I saw St Paul's Cathedral like a tiny speck and Big Ben. What a splendid view, I thought. It's amazing. It's breath taking. Then we were descending to earth, everything returning to its normal size. We were jumping off our carriage, our flight over and heading to the souvenir shop.
"That was great", I said to my family.
"Can we go up again at night when everything is lit up."
I couldn't believe I said that. When I returned home I wrote to my friend. Guess where I went?

Lets get ready to write

First let's practice some word skills….

The use of a few well-chosen adjectives and adverbs will make your writing more interesting…

cute (adjective) baby (noun)

dangerous (adjective) burglar (noun)

beautiful (adjective) princess (noun)

fierce (adjective) dog (noun)

baby (noun) cries (verb) loudly (adverb)

dog (noun) barks (verb) fiercely (adverb)

cat (noun) sleeps (verb) peacefully
                                    (adverb)

BEWARE: Do **not** overload your writing with too many adjectives!

I passed the ~~old crumbling~~ ruined castle.

slowly, carefully

Tom drove (……………) *(adverb)* by the
ruined castle.

Put some suitable adjectives and adverbs in the
blanks…

Tom stared (……………) *(adverb)* at the window of
the (……………) *(adjective)* house.

He opened the (……………) *(adjective)* gate and
walked (……………) *(adverb)* up the path.

He knocked (……………) *(adverb)* on the door but
there was no reply so he ran back (……….)
(adjective)

Keep the tense right

If you start in the past tense keep in the past
tense.
        walk**ed**
**Tom ~~walks~~ up the path and pushed open the
gate. He was…**

Annie can be...

Annie is a very kind and caring girl. She likes dancing and tennis. She is afraid of big dogs and of the creepy old house at the end of her road.

A imable	J	S
B earable	K	T
C ute	L	U
D	M	V
E	N	W
F	O	X
G	P roud	Y
H	Q	Z
I	R eckless	

Creepy old house...

This is a large old house, which is said to be haunted! Its walls are crumbling its windows are broken and the garden is so overgrown with weeds it looks like a jungle.

A wful	J	S
B	K	T
C	L	U
D ingy	M	V
E erie	N	W
F earful	O	X
G hostly	P	Y
H orrendous	Q	Z
I	R	

People can be...

Mean   miserly   selfish   grasping

Stingy   miserable   sneaky   sad

depressed   stupid   foolish   silly

idiotic   crazy   absurd   ridiculous

preposterous   ludicrous   senseless

nonsensical   brainless   irrational   illogical

misguided   fool hardy   reckless   deceitful

horrible   spiteful   unkind   nasty

malicious   cruel   wicked   evil   snappy

beastly   bad   bright   intelligent

respectable   sensible   well groomed   daring

awkward   kind   caring   thoughtful

gentle   helpful   compassionate   loving

considerate   concerned   extrovert

out going   shy   withdrawn   timid

Now describe these people using good adjectives.

(example) the proud professor

boy   man   old man   lad   grandad

uncle   girl   woman   lady   grandma

old woman   spinster   auntie   cousin

baby   child   youngster   youth

professor   teacher   robber   burglar   thief

policeman   fireman   waitress   doctor

nurse   chef   criminal   witch   wizard

Linking Words

The Accident

First   Tom's friend came round to see if he wanted to go on a bike ride.

Soon   they were riding on their bikes through the woods.

Then   it started to rain heavily.

Next   Tom and his friend heard thunder rumbling in the distance.

Suddenly   in his hurry to get home, Tom lost his balance and fell off his bike and hit his head.

Eventually   the ambulance arrived to take Tom to hospital.

Finally   the boys have learnt their lesson.
To always wear a helmet when riding a bike and to take care!

You can see from this simple story that linking words can help you order a story.

<u>Believable Characters</u>
<u>Who are they?</u>………..

<u>Mr Evans</u>

* Well into his sixties
* Rude, speaks abruptly
* Impatient
* Thick white hair at the
   back
* Bald on top
* Well built
* Tall
* How did they meet?………..
* What do they say to each other?……….

<u>Tom</u>
* Nine years old
* Thin, pale

* Bright blue eyes
*…………………..
*…………………..
* What happens?

Describing words for settings...
adjectives

empty   remote   isolated   uninhabited

unoccupied   wild   ghostly   neglected

broken down   gloomy   grimy   chilly

bleak solitary   spine chilling   bare

quiet haunted   dim   dismal   dingy

shadowy   uncanny   murky   pitch black

spidery   creepy   weird   mysterious

eerie   frightening   sinister   precarious

dangerous   risky   hazardous   perilous

unnatural   freezing   exciting   thrilling

noisy   peaceful   beautiful   pretty

---

nouns

woodhouse   forest   mountains hills

countryside   town   city   seaside   marsh

day   night   evening   morning   afternoon

Setting

You don't need too much description just pick out some important details.
Use your senses: sight, hearing, smell, taste and touch.

(example)
I could smell delicious burgers even before I entered the fast food restaurant.
or (turn sentences round for interest)
Even before I entered the fast food restaurant I could smell the delicious burgers.

I could see the mouth-watering burger steaming in the plastic carton. The smell wafted across the shiny tables. The creamy texture of the milk shake slid softly over my tongue. The young people happily chatted together, as they gobbled down huge bags of crispy fries.

Use suitable adjectives and adverbs.
How does this place feel?
What is the atmosphere like?

\

Lets find describing words for weather…

hot   sunny   boiling   sweltering   scorching

sizzling   burning   sun drenched

roasting   baking   blistering   warm   humid

cold   freezing   chilly   chill   shivery

frosty   snowy   bitter   icy   arctic   wintry

nippy   hurricane   tornado   stormy

overcast   windy   blustery   breezy   gusty

blowing hard   pelting with rain   drizzle

down pour   torrential rain   driving rain

shower   misty   foggy

Describe the following words with adjectives...

e.g. The dark, dismal **forest**
     The scorching, hot **sun**

wood   tree   cottage

log   child   house   youth

witch   night   circumstances

fur   atmosphere   shadows

ghost

Characters may be...

Trapped   Buried   Stuck

Hijacked   Life in danger   Falling

Fighting for life   Involved in explosion

Involved in a crash   Caught   Sick   Robbed

Injured   Lost   Shot   Bitten by a snake

Alone   Arrested   Kidnapped

On the run

How do characters feel when the story reaches its climax and characters find themselves in such situations?

Use strong verbs...
Are they – terrified, lonely, petrified, desperate, confused, hopeless, in despair, despondent, forgotten, scared, no way out, no where to turn, useless, shocked, stunned, dazed, sick, scared, confused, hurt, angry, upset, cross, panic...

How do they move? Start, stroll, race, wander
How do they talk? Reply, whisper, shout, scream, yell, stammer, grunt

10 Tips to Remember When Writing

1) The opening sentence makes us want to know what will happen so we want to read on.

2) In the first paragraph you introduce characters, set the scene and start the plot rolling.

3) The middle paragraph will include the main action. A series of events will unfold. Suspense is built up.

4) The ending you choose, whether it be a happy ending, a cliff hanger or a moral ending, will be how you want your reader to feel when he has finished the story.

Structure your story with an opening, development, complication, crisis and resolution.

5) Use dialogue to move the story along where appropriate.

6) Remember to use a variety of sentences, some short, some compound and some complex to make your writing interesting.

7) Use a variety of connectives, also called conjunctions, to enrich your writing. They can be used at the beginning or in the middle of sentences and fall into three groups,

* short words (if, but, then, so, as, if)
*compound words (however, therefore, nevertheless, although)
*more than one word (as a result of, because of)

8) Be aware of tenses! Take care to continue writing in the tense you started with!

Past Tense

Tom knock**ed** on the door.

Grandma slipp**ed** on the banana skin and broke her leg.

Continuous Past - Passive
Continuing to do this even though the next action has happened.

Tom **was knocking** on the door. His friend answer**ed**

Grandma **was running** when she slipp**ed** on the banana skin and broke her leg.

---

9) Use interesting vocabulary (darting fox), astounding adjectives to go with your nouns (enchanting house) and admirable adverbs (he shouted loudly) to accompany your verbs so you avoid boring words, like get, nice and said.

(10) Use interesting figurative language like similes and metaphors to compare…

Similes (use like and as to compare)

A soap slithers **like** a slimy snail leaving a trail of foam down the bath.

Grandad's clothes brush is **like** a greedy hedgehog scampering up and down the cloth looking for morsels of fluff to eat.

Mum drove the car **as** if she was a racing driver in the grand prix.

Metaphors

The hair dryer is a growling dragon breathing out hot air.

Grandad's hosepipe has a sprinkler that is a cool fountain on the lawn on summer nights.

My grandad's bristle clothes brush is a hedgehog scampering up and down the cloth looking for morsels of fluff to eat.

Use some alliteration (Shauna's shiny shell from the seashore.)

Use onomatopoeia - words that sound like they are (bang, crash, crunch.)

Build up Characters
Tom Smith's first day at the new school

Who is Tom Smith?

Where is the new school?

What is his new teacher like?

What does she say to him?

Which children does he meet?

What are their names?

What do they say to him?

How is Tom feeling?

How is he reacting to the situation?

Now, plan a story called First Day at School

Make a Plan

The first paragraph

Tom Smith was an eleven-year-old boy who absolutely hated work. He was quite timid and…
His new school was...
The new teacher was Miss… who was very strict. She decided Tom was a disobedient boy who lacked concentration and did not pay attention. She told him to sit next to Jordan Brown who pretended to be nice at first but actually stole Tom's dinner money to be spiteful. By playtime Tom felt quite upset and longed to go back to his old school.

When you start writing use different words to start each sentence; try and write at least four sentences before you start one with the same word e.g. "he"

The second paragraph

Now think, what happens next?
List the events and build up suspense. Write the last sentence of the second paragraph here in capitals.

In the playground Tom met a different boy called Lewis but he didn't realise he was a friend of Jordan. He (use pronouns – he, she, it, we, you) said things to Lewis about Tom. Jordan and Lewis made a plan to teach the new boy a lesson. Lewis made Tom go onto the climbing frame and the gang cut the rope. He fell. SUDDENLY HE HEARD A SNAP!

The third paragraph

Now wind it up. Make a satisfactory ending. Will the ending be happy or will it be a cliff hanger or have you decided on a tale with a moral. At this stage in your writing write three equal paragraphs.

Tom woke up in hospital. His leg was broken Jordan was expelled from the school and Lewis was excluded. His classmates were sorry for Tom and he made lots of friends.

Decide who the narrator will be. Will it be the 1st or 3rd person?

If you choose to write in the 3rd person your narrator will see everything that goes on, like a fly on the wall. If you choose to write in 1st person you will have to tell the story as you see it through the character.

ALWAYS READ YOUR WORK THROUGH.

KEEP WRITING IN THE SAME TENSE. IF YOU START IN THE PAST TENSE, KEEP TO THE PAST TENSE.

Before you write a published copy read it through again. Check your spelling! Here are some typical spelling mistakes to look out for:

proswaded – persuaded
grabed – grabbed
seam – seem
abbout – about
finaly – finally
spitefull – spiteful
tempreture – temperature

Remember you may get full marks in the spelling test but when you are writing you may get carried away with the story line and not think about spelling. Make sure you remember the spelling rules.

* Longer words ending in the suffix 'full' have one 'l'
e.g. spiteful
Short words have double l

* Words with a short vowel have two consonants.
It is not grabed but grabbed.

* When short vowels are followed by double consonants
the second vowel is stressed.

* In the word 'making' you cannot have an 'e' and an 'i'
together, drop the 'e' to add the 'ing'.
'i' before 'e' except after 'c'

* Remember to get plural endings correct, 'bully' becomes 'bullies', 'half' becomes 'halves', 'fox' becomes foxes.

* Learn the right spelling for homonyms, words that sound the same.
The **seam** on a shirt
It **seems** to me

The wind **blew**
My trousers are **blue**

* Use pronouns. Avoid repetition i.e. "He met a boy called Jordan and Jordan was very spiteful.
Use, "He met a boy called Jordan and he was very spiteful".

* Watch out that you put in correct punctuation; like **apostrophe's** i.e.
<u>Toms</u> first day - <u>Tom's</u> first day

capital letters i.e.
jordan - Jordan

and **speech marks** i.e.
You have some visitors shall I send them in?
"Shall I send them in?" said the nurse,
"Yes please!" said Tom.

* Use full stops or put in connectives.

He asked if Tom wanted a window opened He
sharpened his pencil

He asked if Tom wanted the window opened and
sharpened his pencil.

* Don't start a sentence with but or and.
But Jordan was spiteful.

* Question marks and exclamation marks always come
before the speech marks end.
A new speaker has a new line.

**Take a rough piece of paper. Draw the four
characters in this story. Draw in the setting
add the details from the school, the
playground, the class room…**

Jot down some words for each character...

<u>Jordan</u>

....

spiteful

....

....

....

<u>Teacher</u>

....

....

....

strict

<u>Lewis</u>

....

easily led

....

....

<u>Tom</u>

....

....

timid

Now start to write your first draft using your plan.

The first paragraph

Tom Smith was an eleven year old boy who…
It was his first day at the new school. As he walked in he saw his new teacher Mrs…

The first paragraph will include the details of character and setting.

The second paragraph will list events building up the plot creating suspense and making it exciting.
IT WILL END IN YOUR SUSPENSE SENTENCE!

The third paragraph will wind up the story with your chosen ending.

Remember to always read your work through.
Keep writing in the same tense.
Check your spelling.

The Terrible Day

When you are satisfied with your first draft publish your story by rewriting it or typing it up on the computer.

This story is taken from a draft written by Jo ling (age 10).

Tom Smith was an eleven year old boy who hated work and found it difficult to concentrate. It was his first day at his new school, St Hilda's. As he walked into the crowded classroom, he saw his new teacher Miss Evans. She looked very mean and had monster like eyes. He could tell at once she was going to be stern, strict and snappy. During his first morning she told him off and said he must pay attention and then told him to sit next to a boy at the back of the class. He was called Jordan and seemed really nice when he asked if Tom wanted his pencils sharpened. However, in the dinner hour Tom found out how spiteful his new friend was because he stole his dinner money. The teacher would not listen and Tom had no lunch. He started to feel upset and wished he was back at his old school.

By the time he reached afternoon break, things were getting a bit better. He had made another friend called Lewis. He didn't know that Lewis was a great friend of Jordan. In the last lesson, Jordan whispered a plan to Lewis and they both gave Tom the evil eye. After school everything seemed to be fine. Lewis asked Tom to come and have a look at the swing seat. It was a tyre on the top of a high plank that is attached to a high line and you swing up and down on it. Lewis was persuading Tom to go right up to the top of the plank but Tom was a bit unsure about it. Lewis started to get really impatient and pushed Tom on top of the tyre. Tom didn't manage to reach the tyre but at the last second he grabbed it with the tip of his fingers. Suddenly, he saw Jordan and he was running towards him pulling a shiny object out of his pocket. There was a loud SNAP!

Tom awoke in hospital the next morning. At first he didn't know how he'd got there. He found out he had a plaster cast around his leg. A nurse was taking his temperature, "Oh finally you're awake," she said. "That naughty boy Jordan cut the rope of the swing seat you were sitting on. You fell down and the tyre fell straight onto your leg. It's broken and your kneecap is fractured. That Jordan boy is going to be expelled from the school and that Lewis will be excluded as well. They are two nasty bullies and they deserve to be punished. You have some visitors. Shall I send them in?" "Yes please!" said Tom and his mum and dad walked in.

Your turn now

Write your own stories

Choose from these titles…

Run For Your Life   Trapped
A Frightening Incident   The Surprise
The Creepy Tale   Lost
If Only Pets Could Talk

THINK OF SOME MORE TITLES

What is Creative Writing?

It is writing a story or narrative. The writer uses his imagination to create believable characters, a setting and a plot.
The writer describes what the characters do, what they say and how they react to each other. The narrator implies things about the characters so we feel that we know them.

The writer entertains his reader, through his narrator who tells the story.

He uses words to conjure up a mood so the reader wonders what will happen.
He uses words to create an atmosphere, the characters feelings and emotions, for example, fears, loves or hates so the reader identifies with the characters.

The writer can vary the pace so the story moves fast or slow, building up suspense or tension so the reader has to read on.

The writer chooses who tells the story. He chooses how much to tell the reader and what information about the characters to keep disclosed. The writer gives clues about the characters so the reader can form their own opinion.

The writer has an overall view of events. He structures his writing with a good beginning (opening or introduction). He develops the plot with all its complications and builds up to a crisis and then writes a resolution or ending.
Sometimes they may use flash backs to something said in the past.

Sometimes a story will start at the end and go back in time, recalling events in the past.

Sally Ann Jones, wife of Peter and mother of four children trained as a teacher in the 70's and has since worked as a primary school teacher and private tutor as well as a freelance artist and illustrator. She exhibits her paintings and has published several as greetings cards.

This book is part of a series of educational material she has written based on the needs of the children she tutors.

Her daughter, Amanda, obtained a BA (Hons) in English Language, Linguistics and Sociology at the University of Surrey. She has recently completed an MA.

This book is dedicated to all the children who have tested it with such success.

For practice in Persuasive and Information Writing techniques and for more tips on writing good English and hints on good spelling, punctuation and grammar see the other books in our range.

Made in the USA
Lexington, KY
05 November 2012